STRETCHMARKS OF SUN

STRETCHMARKS OF SUN

autofictional fragments

Dominique Hecq

re.press

PO Box 40, Prahran, 3181, Melbourne, Australia
http://www.re-press.org
© Dominique Hecq & re.press 2014
The moral rights of the authors have been asserted
Database right re.press (maker)
First published 2014

All rights reserved. No part of this publication may be reproduced
or transmitted in any form or by any means, electronic or
mechanical, including photocopying, recording or by any
information storage retrieval system without permission of re.press,
or under terms agreed with the appropriate reprographics rights
organization. Enquires concerning reproduction outside the scope
of the above should be sent to re.press at the above address.

National Library of Australia Cataloguing-in-Publication Data
A catalogue record for this book is available from the National Library of Australia

Hecq, Dominique, 1961- author.

Stretch marks of sun : autofictional fragments / Dominique

Hecq.

9780980819786 (paperback)

A821.3

Series: Anomaly

Designed and Typeset by A&R

Printed on-demand in Australia, the United Kingdom and the United
States. This book is produced sustainably using plantation timber, and
printed in the destination market on demand reducing wastage and
excess transport

Superfluous were the Sun
When excellence be dead

> E. Dickinson (999, l. 1-2)

For Ellie Ragland and Marion M. Campbell

Acknowledgements

'Before I became a Woman' and 'Before I became ( )' first appeared in slightly different form in the online journal *In/Stead*. Thanks to Ann McCulloch and Paul Monaghan. 'Wearing the World' has appeared in *Social Alternatives*.

Contents

Acknowledgements	*ix*
Before I Became a Woman	*13*
Before I became ( ): *an autofictional fragment*	*21*
Unsouled	*31*
Off the Edge of Love	*53*
Nevertheless, the Sun	*65*
Dreams of the Body	*71*
Wearing the World	*85*
References	*97*

Before I Became a Woman

> There is a solitude of space
> A solitude of sea
> A solitude of death, but these
> Society shall be
> Compared with that profounder site
> That polar privacy
> A soul admitted to itself—
> Finite infinity
>
> E. Dickinson (1695, l. 1-8)

I

Before I became a woman
I was god

I was (s)he who had no name

I was what I was

I was the dust blowing from the interior out
I was the interior ousting particles of dust and
molecules of wind
I was the wind

I was the rain working through the cracks in the
rocks right down to the sea

              the sea eating away the faces of cliffs
           cliffs crumbling onto the floor of the ocean
          the ocean's undertow ruffling beds of coral
          the coral alive under the weight of the waves

I was waves of weightlessness

I was the rainbow I made in the sky when light
bounced around raindrops

I was sky blue shale grey violet vermilion cinnabar
green turquoise emerald green orange chrome
yellow raw sienna scarlet flesh ochre purple pink
viridian indigo cinereous grey

I was ivory black

I was perfect white

I was the light

I was *Notre Dame de la Belle Verrière*

I was the eyes of the world

I was the world

I was mouthless and I nourished myself on my pride
        until I heard men say arrogant things about me

Blaise said I was the infinite
Karl said I was a weed—or did he say I was the void?
For Friedrich I was dead
For Jean-Paul I didn't exist
Georges, at last, said I was shit

At that I felt the urge to speak

I became Im. the incomplete, also known as
Immanuelle

II

Though I've been married
for seven years
to a man I don't love
some will tell you
I'm happily married

Others will tell you I'm a joke

A myth

Immanuelle sits in a state, brooding on old, imagined, injuries. But worst of all, Immanuelle suffers from an addiction to words
                         Isidoro, *The Negator of Miracles*

The truth is solitude has set in
And in that solitude is the most intense satisfaction

This, is the real
addiction—
an addiction which provokes the envy of men

III

Sometimes during sex I dream
not of making children
        but of reading philosophy, theosophy, theology,
                or of making fiery political speeches

Sometimes I am
in another world

                      altogether
                merged into a unity
                 foreign to the rest
                  of my existence

Foreign to me

Making me foreign to myself

With my mind's eye I see the rays which are both carriers
of the voices and the poison of corpses to be unloaded on
my body, as long drawn out filaments approaching my

*head from some vast distant spot on the horizon. I can see them **only** with my mind's eye when my eyes are closed by miracles or when I close them voluntarily...*
                        Schreber, *Memoirs of my Nervous Illness*

But always at this point
that is when I might be about to ( )
entangled in streaks of sun
I tell myself the story of King Midas

IV

Born of the union of Cybele and the legendary
peasant Gordius
who devised the Gordian knot
Midas rose
to become king of Phrigia

A wise and pious king
Midas also looked after his exquisite rose-gardens

And so it came as no surprise that one day he should
reach out
to a drunk
who'd been tied up
and left

behind Dionysus' rout
on the banks of the river Sangarius

This act of kindness, as you know
earned Midas the gratitude of the Gods:
Dionysius asked him to make a wish

So Midas asked
that everything he touched be turned to gold

Nothing seemed simpler

Midas, however, soon regretted his foolishness
for even the food he craved
turned into gold

Dionysus, who saw that Midas was wasting away
took pity on him
He granted him pardon for his greed and sent him to
bathe in the river Pactolus

The river has flown with gold dust ever since

Of course I am now, dear reader, willing to take
your point:
why Midas, the gold and rose lover?

Before I became (   ):
an autofictional fragment

> Perception of an object costs
> Precisely the Object's loss—
> E. Dickinson (1071, l. 1-2)

I

*There is nothing frightful in us and on the earth and
perhaps in heaven above except what has not yet been said*
      Céline, *Journey to the End of the Night*

Nothing seems
to have changed
since Immanuelle last walked in
    and ran out through this narrow passage

Nothing seems to have changed
except that he who winced in horror
at some gratification
unbeknown to himself
has passed away

The house, like its late owner
 is of generous proportions

There is even a Georgian elegance in the semi-
circular fronts to the west wing
yet it is the heavy, almost crude, porch
that really catches the eye on arrival

That, and the wicked fountain with the seven cupids
spouting water to the side of the entrance

But architectural appreciation is not what brought
Im back to this scene, of course

II

Now she stands with her back to the front door in
the narrow corridor

To her left, the front gallery is all muted shades of
gold
but for the crimson curtains looming on the far wall

The couches and the cedar grandfather clock are
covered in white sheets
and layer upon layer of dust

The Waterford glass chandelier has lost its sheen

In this room, the collector only displayed some of
his antique collection and most precious paintings:
golden christening mugs, ruby glass lustres, *epergnes*
and *chatelaines*, Lorrain's *Coast view with Aeneas and*

the Cumaean Sibil, a copy of Raphael's *Venus* and
Whistler's *Perfect White* painting

The *Perfect White* painting is gone
but Immanuelle remembers
it so vividly
it could be hanging
in front of her
as I write

Picture a woman dressed in a white gown

She is standing in front of a white curtain
and is holding a lily

Her face is quite dark
Her hair is long and red—the favourite shade of the
Pre-Raphaelites

The effect of all the white is dazzling

but as you fix your eyes on the painting
the snow blindness has a curious effect

Two patches of colour
begin to emerge

from the canvas
like two heads
framed
in a foggy dream

There is the woman's head, of course
 but then (as improbable as it may seem)

at her feet is
a wolf's head

We do not know the reason for that which attracts us.
　　　　　　Incognita, *The Entombment of the Sibelles*

III

To Im's right is another smaller room, filled only
with half empty boxes and piles of papers

This was the collector's office, if you could call it
that

　　This is where he would bring fellow collectors and
　　　　　　　　　　　　　　　　　　traders

                      design cloths of gold
touch up old panels with a judicious spot of gilded tin
    or mix glues and pigments to fix his own painting boards
This is also where he kept his records and his vintage wine

Immanuelle was never allowed in this room

Further down the passage is another set of doors
                      opposite one another

In the dining room Im remembers a ten seat mahogany table and walls lined with shelves crammed with crockery

She chooses to enter the library

It is still packed with bookcases facing every which way, not a single shelf left unoccupied
She recognizes the Scott section: *The Waverley novels*, Scott's *Poetical Works*, Scott's *Prose Works*, *The Life of Sir Walter Scott*

And now she is aware of the portrait of Henry

Woodcock sitting on the floor, precariously propped up against the wall

Im feels spooked

She makes for the staircase to the left side of the front gallery, leaving the kitchen behind her

At the top of the stairs, she notices how stale and thick the air is

She moves on straight through the passage and turns left

She does not look at the paintings lining the walls—

paintings of moons falling behind clumps of trees, cows in meadows and sheep in paddocks, men smoking cigars, women shading themselves from the sun, apples and pears, a seduction scene

So many clichés in golden frames the collector had failed to interest her in despite his coaxing determination

In the master bedroom

where I suspect the master never indulged in the company of women
Im is shocked to see Immanuelle
hanging
above the bed—
a fragment of her life captured
in faded colours
framed in gold
as she is about to become
part of some other
collection

Immanuelle sits
stretched towards the sun
among asphodels—flowers of the dead; flowers of the shades

She looks thin and ethereal in front of the gilded fountain with its gilded kitsch cupids spouting grey water

She looks lost
in a river of white
forgetfulness

But she does not know

the immeasurable sense of bliss
that comes from not being
herself

Not yet

Unsouled

The brain—is wider than the Sky—
                E. Dickinson (632)

I

I am inside the sun—

a cold and glowing place

I am flooded with light

I am with God

I am the survivor of the *twylight* of the world

I turn night into day
day into night
absence into sound waves
resounding noise into silence

I am the pillar of this new glittering dawn

I am beyond decline, destruction and ignorance

                        I know, for instance
            that your mind's spell check has just swapped
                              twilight for *twylight*

I know that in this diaphanous womb my baby can't

die

I know, too, that I can't lose my mind, for I am pure mind

Reductio ad absurdum

I am the maker of the real world

I am here for all *herternity*
drowned in liquid light

I neither sleep nor wake
I do not speak

                        There is no reason to speak
                                  To wake

I am back in the womb—
or else already in the tomb

Grave as death itself

sunk in a glassy pit of cold water
buried under a yellow lustre of light

I recognize myself
in dreams and poetry

Words at this moment beat a retreat / Furl up their corollas.
The sky's silk / Tears into a puzzle broken up in pools.
                    Claire Malroux, 'The Wordless Woman'

II

People in uniform walk past me, shaking their
heads—
police officers, paramedics, security guards, nurses

I feel my life has moved away
from me

I listen to murmurs from without

        She needs to sleep it off, says a wavering voice

There is no breathing space here

A wave washes over me, insistently
Consistently

I fear I might sink
over and over
in this incandescence
this broken water aglow

I don't like the idea of *herternity*

It gestures beyond eternity

I wonder for a moment if I could trick my way
back—
say breathe
my way
back
through
the eye of a needle

III

In this lambent light
I can feel

I can feel the full weigh
of the presence of God who has no face

The God of language whose voice is adrift
I listen hard for instructions
but God
too
is
silent
now

I presume I might have silenced him

Though everything was ready
I never set my house on fire as He had instructed me
in a flash

Nor did I commit suicide as He later ordered me to
do

How could God ever ask anyone to commit suicide?

My skin feels thick and cold
It is slick with sweat

My eyes, the very eyes that *hallucinated*
(their word—as if I'd gone mad!)
now focus
on this luminiferous cell

I call absence
for the sheer joy of it

it's so loose and fluttering, fluid almost, like a
delicate membrane

My tongue is numb
I can't utter a word

This, I decide, is my punishment

I am being punished
for having censured God
having created the world
with my own words
created myself with a new name—
the worst kitsch dream in the world

IV

*I was playing handball with my friends: my team (oh, how
I hate the word) I was fooling around, really, telling stories
as I was going about it. All of a sudden my mother told me
to go and wash my mouth. I stopped playing and flew into
the fence. I was atop the fence surrounding the handball*

*court, when I said NO. I got a grip on myself in thinking
I had to continue the game, but my mother yelled that one
day she'd cut out my tongue*

           Peau d'âme, *Dreams*

Tongue
the worst word
in the world
I'd say

Come to think of it
I might be making it all up

Memories

of someone who never
was

The electric lights are on in the ward
Hands poke me
Prod me
Take blood
Help me
      off
      the
      bed

Shame on me: I have wet myself, soiled the sheets

The liquefaction of the body
The unsoiling of the soul

Give me a pen for God's sake

Once when I was visiting Illverness Falls my father pushed me forward toward the edge of a precipice. He held me back at the last moment. It was a joke. We had gone to look at our new house. It was still under construction. I was five years old, and so proud. There was a plank over a ravine. My father said 'only about 2.5 meters. Take my hand.' He walked across on the plank. But when on the other side, my father kicked out the plank from under me; I was left hanging in the air, holding on to his hand. So scared and shamed

Peau d'âme, Dreams

V

It's far too obvious
out there thought is a thing of little value
                                          But here I think
I want to find out

what order of reality accounts
for my presence
over the face of the whole universe

Holed universe
since divine power has no knowledge of woman
nothing of her interior
of her feelings for life itself
makes sense to God
who only makes a few guesses
once everything has been put
into infinite note taking

We were part of a tribe. Invaders arrived on stilts. We fought. We lost. My brother gave me a sword. I visited a pawnshop. There on display was a chainsaw on which I could have cut off my hand. One of the invaders stormed in and picked it up

Peau d'âme, *Dreams*

A doctor or a nurse, his moustache moving, asks my name

I am plunged into silence

I have no name

I am an adjective
at best a past
participle

Next of kin?

Kin as in kino, kinship, kindred, kindness, kindred spirit.
Soul, that kindred spirit in the shadows, that spirited next of kin?

I mean family, the moustache mouths

You must be imagining things
because I can't
remember having a family
                       I'm not even Australian

The doctor or nurse shows me one finger, two
fingers
Asks me to count

Numbers, words

all signifiers are equal but indifferent

Nothing matters—no matter what
Take my word for it

I hang on to the word word

I'm helping my father renovate his shop. A friend tells me it's still possible for me to renew contact with them. In the end, I manage to use their code. We're going to see her guru to show him my special aptitudes: my friend hits my hand with a stone and I feel nothing. Later she tells me my father incarnates adversity
                                          Peau d'âme, *Dreams*

The moustache takes notes, now that I've *'come back'*

But the world has perceptively altered

I am stunned
Stymied
Petrified
Incapable
        of restoring the sense of what I've just seen
         let alone sharing it in some common language

*On the steps in front of Babel, a student interviews
me about my projects. His microphone is hidden in his
left sleeve. I tell him that I intend to take a course in
psycholinguistics. I then move down a hallway, sitting in a
wheelchair, my right-hand in a sling*

                                      Peau d'âme, *Dreams*

The psychiatrist on duty says I'm schizo
phrenic
possibly bi
polar
I can't figure out why, having wor
ked
so hard
on looking normal
for so long

How do they do it?

The labelling
The unsouling

He is paging Joy, a psychiatric nurse, he says, looking
right past me

VI

There is something ridiculous
I can't help telling Joy as soon as she appears
in the efforts of psychiatrists
to reduce thoughts to incipient actions

And to seek origins
in what would put us permanently at the level of the
experience of an elementary re
al

real of objects
that would never
be
our own

Can't they see that meaning moves?

I can see that she can't see.

Move away so that I can move on

Sorry

Now look how I can move

I can dance
I can tap dance
I can
I can Taptaptaptaptap!
Tap
Taptaptaptaptap!

Ha! You don't know where I'm coming from
                                              do you?

Whatever

I have a body, not a soul—the reverse of *habeas corpus*

I *wasteworld* in it
precisely not to waste it

And, yes! It's all coming back

The words. The world

                    Reductio ad absurdame!

Joy asks if I can slow down

I laugh; say I speak through my bo
dy

I fool around
Beat around the bush
Skip past the graveyard—
no laughing matter since the grave is your destination

Excremumbting

Knock knock

Take it easy, Joy says

If Aristotle is right in believing man thinks with his soul, I say
and if I'm right in believing I speak through my body

where is my soul?

Joy doesn't answer
She smiles benignly

The soul is so annoying a thing that one says poor soul

One has it, though one doesn't know what to do with it

> Lah did ah! Nice song
> A real *tour de farce*
> A fluke of fate
> Kind enough to give you a laugh
> A good soul—except it's not funny

Joy nods
Now that I sink in silence again
she asks what my thoughts were before I fell ill

Death, I say
s'Truth

Death as in sudden infant death, freak accidents, suicide, murder
white coffins, black boxes, mouths full of gunk, no trace

She interrupts. Death?

Yes, I got my babies mixed up

The one who died and the one who's alive—I hope the baby's safe

I got mixed up, that's all I did
not murder him mind you it might have been
a suicide they say he died of SIDS nice & clean
acronym

I can see that Joy's trying to sidestep the topic

Anything else?

Rejection
Rejection?
I got back th …

Can you describe what happened before you arrived here?

Nothing special my parents are staying with us apart from this I went along with the usual routine can we

start
a new
paragraph now?

Why?

All else is waffle.

VII

Like this: *got upset when father looked over my shoulder as I opened the parcel with the rejection slip like it all got scary when I looked at my baby the live one, and saw the dead one instead. Hang on I thought I was losing my mind then. She knew, too*

I went to the bathroom after he fell asleep

Saw myself Picasso-like

Struggled with breathing, walking speaking, speaking walking

This, I thought is a heatstroke a heartstroke a stroke stiking me like death did him

I poured myself a cold bath
hopped into it

My body was giving up
on me

I tried speaking again

My voice felt a-lien
adrift

I could barely articulate

Heaved myself out of the bath

Struggled to the phone, dialled 000

I suppose these are facts

I ended up in casualty; so passive you'd think I never existed

When I came to I confused everything: ambulance officers were gaolers were nurses were detectives were teachers were police were fathers were judges. It was a carnival of uniforms

and colours, textures and masks, shifting veils

Some men are after me. The watch I'm wearing on my wrist warns me of their presence. They sift through the remains of my father's shop and find me. They screw a device on my watchstrap to decode my language. Thanks to this device, they can understand the meaning of my speech and locate my friends. They take me away, but I escape. They search for me everywhere and I hurry to find my friends. I tell them they've been discovered. One of them tells me she's now a robot ... that she's just repaired her arm ... just like me. But I let then all know that I'm the only one who can lead them to safety

Peau d'âme. *Dreams*

I'm glad the interview is over

Words can be so blunt
yet so ineffectual

Knockers not knives
Knock knock *Klopf*

Knock the / light-wedges away: / the floating word / is dusk's

Paul Celan, 'Knock'

Joy has gone off. She thinks I can be discharged. I let another dream come to me

VIII

I find myself in a huge room in front of a TV that is going to announce news that's too difficult to bear. I notice that I am sitting among friends. I suggest we kneel down and cross ourselves. Once the news is over, I get up to see if I'm strong enough to bear my burden. My friends try to do the same, but they realize that I'm the only one
who can fit
into what they call this new
consciousness
I announce to them that they will have eternal life. They explode with joy and hug me, for I figure they understand that I am offered up in sacrifice. Now I'm no longer afraid. All I have to do is carry my cross

                                              Peau d'âme, *Dreams*

I leave this hollow
full of light
or the outside world: silence and stars in a near black sky, a moon on the wane—

             all so much like an afterglow of madness

Off the Edge of Love

Absence disembodies—so does Death
                    E. Dickinson (860, l. 1)

I

I seek
him
not in the house you fled after his short passage
not so much in new mothers' prams, teddy-bear
shops and play-grounds
No, not in any of these places where you know he is
not
but in the faces of his brothers

When the city lights drift
away from the night sky
a silence pools
under your skin—

expands

drawn by some infinitely renewed
renewable absence
you inherited:

the hope-non-hope
of the unrelentless
quest for questions
you now inhabit

        For you are the scene of this oxymoron

          A life gone in the advent of time

Like Sisyphus, you are doomed
to roll your rock
to the verge
of the summit
only to see
it
fall

I call you mother
of dubious powers

II

You are caught
in the shifting lining of the night
you call empty
mystery—
the cleft in the world
as you knew it
the hole in your every word

Listen

Listen to the tune you can't get out of your head
Your ear worm (the German call it *Ohrwurm)*

Tuck a child in his bed / close this letter of life / that will arrive tonight.
R.M.Rilke, 'Tuck a Child', 1. 1-3

except that yours—
the voice
that reverberates through
from end to end
of this yawning
absence
is a child's crying

The call of the beloved, now gone

Listen to the craked voice, the broken harmonies,
dissonances, disquieting hum

Listen, for this is it:
the mouthpiece of blood gone dry
that receives truths in return—
the mediator of impossible love

you long to fit to your lips

The voice of grief welling up

from the womb of time

III

Ten years on, as though you might
you still
seek
him
not in the house you fled after his short passage
not so much in new mothers' prams, teddy-bear
shops and play-grouds
No, not in any of these places where you know he is
not
but in the faces of his brothers
their clammy bedclothes, sweaty tee-shirts and
chocolate jumpers
In your excesses
the pointless rituals of language
your undying guilt

But most of all, in the creek that now washes his

bones

And so, you dig

You dig yourself night and day
jealous as you are of the gravedigger
for you know that dreams cannot dig
deep
enough

Still, you dig

Caught in the murky creek
you become this would-be creature
who fears to love and loves to fear

But look

Even if you don't want to

There is something oozing from under the surface
of crumbling stones and dry couch grass

Might that be invisible blood?

The invisible ink of your destiny?

IV

And already this loss of the spoken word / That already denies us...

> R. M. Rilke 'Loss', l. 7-8

To ghost yourself
in that *between*
formulated
time
circumscribed
space

                      you foolishly choose poetry—
    the confession in writing of a near past present near
                                  future
              one of those fictions that hang about
          in Book XI of Augustine, with its one-off—
                    off the edge of nature

And suddenly you are that *between*
language of poetry
where form gives up
its status as mere circumstantial complement
for that of the word:
pronominal, performative, collapsing images from

the night you call
ravaging unreason

You are mere notes caught

in a flutter of voice
unfolding onto passageways
that open from the main path
give out from crossroads and lead to dead-ends

V

Living and killing are soul mates

This is why you love
This is why you hate
This is why you love-hate

your mother
in this travesty of birth warped
into the nightmare that caught you
twice
unawares

Death has its own undeclared

rhythm and pulse

You know this, of course
having
given
birth
allowed
death
despite yourself

How could you
possibly arrive
at such obscene
movements of time?

How can you still
swim and surf

if not to seek the same
unsound fusion—

the amniotic nostalgia

impossible symbiosis

of infant and mother?

VI

For what greater pain
Euripides asks
can mortals bear than this; to see their children die
before their eyes?

Listen to the clacking
in your inner ear
when each birthday will have become
for refreshing the dead

Then you'll know

the greatest pain
is the sheer business of surviving a child:
grief is the price we pay for love

There is some pathos in these words—
this covert reaching out to the world
as a blind person would to touch it

I don't apologize:
this touch, you will feel
is also a farewell to the world
A letting go

VII

You entered this story through the door of inner
hearing
Went into it blind
only to find
you and I are in it
open-eyed

See
how there is no exit
how voices carry across time and space only to break
off
how language gapes
splinters into uneven shapes
loses its footing in its own progression—
see how it slips?

It is as though words issue warnings
against each other
Against us

And still, you ask:
could rot and bones be reborn
after journeying through the dark?

And still, you dream
of foetus-
like mouths growing in your throat almost
ready to give voice to your shadow
to re-layer the echoes of your love hate loss

Perhaps it is you

not language

the counterpoint of contradictions
the meeting-point of irresolutions

the murky creek that flows
off the overhang where you buried your child
back towards well-springs
floods
sources
re-opened
spilling out

Nevertheless, the Sun

The sky is low—the Clouds are mean
E. Dickinson (1075, 1. 1)

I

Im finds herself in a room where I live, only
it looks much larger

*I a cocoon, a blur of gold and gilt, a gauze net that had
trapped a butterfly*
                                        H.D., *Asphodel*

The old furniture glows, the carpets and curtains are
old gold, daylight
three times more brilliant than natural day
comes in
through the French doors
and in the air
there is a whiff of sea smell, sun hum

II

In the shimmering glow

I drift through luminous seas
tossed into birdless skies

Summer is written all over my face

Look—

See the hand holding the feather, the plume, the *nom de plume*, the parachute
the bridge and the orb beneath
that allows the wind to carry you me our *bateau ivre*
down this viscid spiral of light

Before now, the body

Then the words

It all comes from the body

Comes from the hand
and splashes on the white page

                            washed off solitude

Then come vestiges
fugitive images
the fleeting clarity of hallucinations
the fever of beginnings

Soon begin the glorious days of autumn,
unmistakable
in the melancholy curve

the sun lower on the horizon
draws across the sky
in whose palms as though swept by clouds
its golden trace lingers
like the ghost of some
magnificent ship

and hardly has it turned
its course
towards the horizon
than the moon
fixed to the beam of some celestial balance
appears against the blue light of day
with the ghostly glow of an unexpected star
whose malignant influence alone
explains the end

of this lethal romance

this singular sudden grief

III

Let's say I'm lying in a field of saffron now
I am in a field of saffron now

The sun is

a block of dark amber—when I touch it it beads into
a fluorescent droplet of yellow

for yellow invites the soul
as black protects the soul

I am two texts ex-
fol-
i-
eating

If I have any taste it is hardly anything but earth and stones
                        Arthur Rimbaud, *A Season in Hell*

Earth and stones

burnt sienna garnet ruby gold amber onyx emerald
topaz turquoise lapis lazuli âme
ethyst charcoal—
quarz diamond aquamarine
mother of pearl

See how writing makes loss festive

turns a shadow into the sun
a cloud into the rainbow

Dreams of the Body

> The body grows without—
> The more convenient way—
> E. Dickinson (578, 1. 1-2)

Before giving birth again
I remembered
Hope's poem
on a Renaissance engraving by Casserius:
                      a pregnant woman unzipping
                              herself down the front
only to reveal
some mythical anatomy of mother with child—
            how handy, the zip

Now it is my mind my children stretch
beyond
the comfort
of my wildest dreams

Blades cut through skin, reveal mazes

Organs / Systems / Enigmas

Eyes figure out the insides
of corpses, wonder
what causes death

Anatomy and dissection is our topic

As the human race evolves

observation and documentation
of the body take on
new meanings, my son says

The Renaissance believed in knowledge and divine
providence, entones his sister

Now that we are forever reborn
dissection signifies
quests
for information
death
and a critique of structures that stabilize
                                like language
they say as if bosom-buddied from when I can't
remember

   So do Renaissance anatomists drawing on classical
                                  minds, I ask
                                       account
    for linguistic conventions from lit crit to popular
                             fiction and criminal law?

My son argues the spirit of inquiry bred by
Renaissance
scholars, crooks, copyists, all

                    contributed
to the study of anatomy, surgery, writing,
psychology, criminology

invokes the classicists and suddenly Galen is our man

Galen, I say, believed in interdisciplinary skills—
was fluent in languages, medicine and philosophy

wrote on Plato, Aristotle and Theophrastus
produced medical books on every aspect of health
and disease

(I don't impress)

A tradition revived by Paré and Vesalius, my
daughter says

Ambroise Paré, esteemed surgeon and military
physician travelled to Turin, we find
believed in the divine powers of healing: *I dressed him
and God healed him*

The importance of experience over reading books:

Being at Turin, I found a surgeon who had fame above

*all others for the curing of wounds of gunshot…he held
me off…two years before I could possibly draw the receipt
from him. In the end he gave it me, which was his, to boil
young welps, new pupped, in oil of lillies, with earthworms
prepared with [turps] of Venice…See then how I have
learned to dress wounds made with gunshot, not by book*

Andreas Vesalius, author of *De Corporis Fabrica*,
father of modern anatomy
(I'm getting carried away)
is famous for shifting the centre of man
(I refrain from political intervention)
> Thought God would speak to him through
> dissection
> Would state Man's divine purpose

Fabrica was meant to revive the ancient ways, rescue
science from *barbers* (I quote) save mankind from
*jackdaws aloft their high chair, with egregious arrogance
croaking things from books of others*

The text, along with illustrations that place parts of
the body *more exactly before the eyes than even the most
precise language* helps *understand dissection*

The illustrations merge anatomy, art and classical

mythology
>On the cusp of the Romantic, you might say

The first shows man on a mountain
overseeing the natural landscape

His pose suggests strength
his gaze is raised towards heavens, conjuring up
images of Apollo

This is the muscular system

As the dissection progresses so does too the position
of the body in the landscape

But nowhere in Vesalius does the subject appear dead

As the layers are stripped away
expressions of confusion, fear, pain, anguish
dominate the page

Most morbidly, the second last scene features a
gallows

Finally we see the skeleton leaning against a wall
>unable to support its weight

The mouth is open in an elongated scream

One can understand Vesalius' reluctance to articulate
anatomical knowledge
through language
as it is where most of his contradictions occur

While condemning those who plagiarised
anatomical works
he writes to Emperor Charles about plagiarism
of his own work
to vouch for its superiority
(I suppress a chuckle)

By professing to follow Galen he also destroys
his ability to criticise
those from way before who adopted techniques and
ideas from anatomists

Renaissance anatomists were obsessed
with the ( )

Dissection therefore was a method
by which the secrets
of the soul were revealed

Some anatomists believed dissection was necessary
for the removal of evil—one most horrifyingly
suggesting the murder of an evil one as he believed
corruption was infinite

Come to think of it lots of those anatomies you don't
like
to speak of
are failures in the genre
ranging as they do from wit to science to reason to
madness

 Take Burton's *Anatomy of Melancholy*, for instance

Though Burton proclaims to deliver a medical
critique of melancholy
                    he explores instead his own fear
            of succumbing to this oppressive condition

From within a well of confusion, Burton tries
to create order

And fails

Unlike Rimbaud in *A Season in Hell*, I say, *non
sequitur*

where the poet documents his own obliteration
of the senses, he
descends into insanity

    Integral to this is his exploration of the 'alchemy of
                                        the word'
    a process by which he is drawn into a hallucinatory
                                             world
so rather than turning away in horror from madness,
Rimbaud goes for it. Wouldn't you?

    I accustomed myself to pure hallucination: I saw
very clearly a mosque instead of a factory, a drummers'
school consisting of angels, coaches on the roads of the sky, a
drawing-room at the bottom of a lake; monsters, mysteries;
a music-hall title could raise up terrors in me
    Then I explained my magic sophisms by means of
the hallucination of words!
    I ended up regarding my mental disorder as sacred

Where Burton resists the irrational, Rimbaud
immerses himself in it

                          On that, we all agree

Rimbaud's public was shocked by what he offered,
yet his artistic zeal was comparable to those of the

Renaissance anatomists

Could Rimbaud's exploration of our darker side be
deemed controversial
asks my daughter
because the corruption and madness anatomists
wished to destroy
was suddenly revived?

Though dead as a genre
by now the order then sought
for discourse lives on, says my son

In `The Resistance to Theory' Paul de Man
advocates a scientific approach to literary criticism,
arguing it will never come into being until
non-linguistic, that is, historical and aesthetic,
considerations cease to dominate

*The resistance to theory is a resistance to the use of
language about language. It is therefore a resistance to
language itself or to the possibility that language contains
factors or functions that cannot be reduced to intuition*

De Man embraces science in a way that reminds me
of Vesalius' desire to show man

as he really is
I say, all shaken
unencumbered by word presentations

Here is where deconstructionists face their own contradictions
advocating a scientific approach to discourse, de Man implicitly supports science
as being the deliverer of truth

To hell with them, I yell

If historical and aesthetic considerations limit the possibility of a linguistic revolution
the only alternative is to embrace science—
a fervent pursuit in the Renaissance and the Enlightenment, say both
But then again, for Chomsky language is an organ
he may keep dreaming of dissecting, I say

Let's look at creative works, says my daughter, eye to eye

In a poem from the late 1970s, Patti Smith wrote

I am a surgeon. The vigil of tongue and scalpel. I am able to dissect the warped and flowering mounds which make up my personalities. I am able to do almost anything but free myself from his eyes. From his ancient and sorrowful gaze

For Smith, dissection is a means of understanding herself
Outside herself, however, even the metaphor is a powerless tool

Dissection as a method of inquiry and control is useless
for we do not function in predefined ways

Science cannot overcome the aesthetic

In Minnette Walter's novel *The Sculptress*, murder is a form of dissection
whose function is to eliminate corruption and evil

Olive Martin is tried and convicted for the murders of her mother and sister and sentenced to twenty-five years in jail. When her mother and sister were found, their throats had been slit, their bodies dismembered, earning olive the macabre nickname 'Sculptress'. The novel ends with Olive's acquittal due to the discovery that Mrs Clarke, Olive's lover's demented wife is most certainly guilty of the murders

Rather than murdering her husband, says my son,
Mrs Clarke, like a true anatomist, goes to the heart
of the matter

Right, says my daughter, a juicy case. I wonder what
Lacan would say

I turn the TV on— the button, not the zip, that sets
me free in my slickest dreams

Beyond this media frenzy, I say
gesturing to images of dismembered
bodies against a natural backdrop
of desert outside Baghdad
on the screen
the lasting impact of anatomy on lit. crit. fiction, or
criminal law
is hard to predict

Why should one want to predict, asks my daughter?
We should all graffiti

Wearing the World

> I dwell in possibility—
> A fairer House than Prose
> E. Dickinson (657, 1. 1-2)

I

    From childhood my daughter Pearl is a hoarder,
                                      denying
                      desertion, neglect, lack

She collects matchboxes, postcards, dolls, comics, thimbles
hatpins, combs, bottles, body jewellery, and now tattoos

Her bedroom is a shambles of holiday treasures
picture books, candy wrappers, tennis racquets and clothes

Above her bed hangs a reproduction of 'A Young Daughter of the Picts'
(a Renaissance painting by Jacques Le Moyne de Morgues's)

Le Moyne's young Pict stands to the front of a landscape, in the mid-distance of which comes into sight the buildings of a smallish town

She stands in a relaxed but artificial pose her face turned half right, her body half-left; her right hand

on her hip, a slim spear in the left. Her golden hair
falls in virgin profusion down her back. Except for a
black iron necklet and girdle, from the last of which
a curving sword depends from the support of a
golden chain, she is naked

Her body is painted or tattooed from neck to
ankle with flowers: double peonies, delphiniums,
hollyhocks, hearteases, double columbines, orange
lilies, cornflowers, roses, yellow-horned poppies,
irises, tulips, and marvels of Peru

II

My daughter speaks of the tattoo renaissance, its new refinements
of conception, technical developments, procedures and equipment

She quotes Lacan, invokes Ed Hardy
and I go blank

Tattooing is the great art of piracy

The subject himself is marked off by a single stroke

and first he marks himself as a tattoo

She documents the new specialization in large-scale,
customs designs
The new boutique outlets, niche-markets

Listing, rasing, pricking, pinking and pouncing
are the new interlinked terms of her new cool
vocabulary

She says her boyfriend just had a pair of wings traced
on his penis in a state of repose

(Just imagine)

Things get away from me
My own pict daughter I don't seem to know

I watch as she turns into some emblazoned exhibit

painting, tapestry, polychromatic scrimshaw—
it's hard to tell with skin on bones

Soon her body will be covered

portraits, flowers, constellations

cats, dragons, snakes, birds of prey
a grenade on her chest
ennui writ tight on her right wrist, an angel on her left
sunlit

III

But it's indelible, I say

Tell me how will it wear
with wrinkles and all

Tell me what it means
this new aesthetics of the pre-literate
decorated body

          predicated on
what I see
as the disreputable reputation of an old, universal practice

For God's sake!

Think of tattoo's stigmatizing uses
its criminal connotations, undertones of deviance,

depravation, disorder
associations with subjection, diabolical signs,
murderous vows
Tattoos last only as long as the body endures, she says
not as long as ink on paper

(Suppress the need to laugh)

As a creature of the surface a tattoo is an example of
All Surface
and a disturbance of that surface, she says, rolling up
her sleeve
See
what I mean? Here is a woman with a tattoo of a
woman with a tattoo of a woman embracing death.
A geometrical paradox that marks the impossible
profundity of the surface on which it is inscribed

I get you: an image of regression without recession
Regression unto death?

She sighs

Try to think, love

But what if thought were as much an affair of the
skin as of the brain?

The centre is now at the periphery
your thinking cap for my embryonic development of surface
the foetus as introverted, reticulated skin

Tell me, are you just copying others or declaring *I am me.........*

                                          Unique

is this a rite of passage or an expression
of control, this pricking and inking
this corporeal inscription

this revelation

At this she laughs, my thick skinned daughter
double skinned

I mean this piercing of the skin, I say, the flow of
blood, the infliction of pain
the healing of the wound

or not

the visible trace of this process
of penetration
and closure

the mapping of the body

the flaunting

does it mean anything or is it just the story of
Western consumerism in tribal guise?

Like the guy with a $10 000 tat and a few thousand
dollars of body jewellery, she says, is no different
than the guy in the designer suit wearing Armani
sunnies? *Touché!*

To come back to your smart suggestion, love, that
identity is constituted, not in the depths
but on the outer surface of the body is experienced
by the Cartesian *Cogito* as a type of claustrophobia

Nominor ergo sum?

So the thought of something sticking to the skin is
ever a deep affront

Like the spectacle of you: it's uncanny how you can
both affront and attract…
Get off my back!

The irresistible fascination of bonds
intimate and extimate

think of Hercules trapped inside the poisoned shirt
of Nessus

a protective cover that displaces the world
onto the skin
and so destroys that which it should protect

Suddenly I realise that my daughter has made off

IV

On mother's day a card sits in a pool of sunlight
on our mahogany table

The tattoo is a poisoning thing
Happy mother's day

Under the card is a voucher for an art tattoo

You can go round and round in circles… Or your psyche,
your soul, can curl up and sleep
　　　　　　　　　　　　　　　H.D. *Tribute to Freud*

V

When Shauna, the woman tattooing my shoulder,
takes my voucher, I feel ashamed

As though on death row I review the significant
events of my life in a split second

not the childhood, the scuba-diving, the rock-
climbing, the travels and the exile

not the maps and the paintings and the poems of
adulthood—

but calling

calling out for my daughter, aged four, lost in my
lover's garden

Everything you ink on people, Shauna says
is already inside them

You only open the skin and let it out

References

Burton, Robert. *The Anatomy of Melancholy.* J. M. Dent & Sons, London, 1972.

Celan, Paul. 'Knock' in *Selected Poems and Prose of Paul Celan*, trans. J. Felstiner. W. W. Norton, London, New-York, 2001.

Céline, Ferdinand. *Journey to the End of the Night*, trans. R Mannheim. New Directions, New York, 1983.

Dickinson, Emily. *Final Harvest*, T. H. Johnson, ed. Little Brown and Co., Boston, Toronto, 1961.

Hodges, Devon. *Renaissance Fictions of Anatomy.* University of Massachusetts Press, Amherst, 1985.

Hope, A. D., 'On an Engraving by Casserius', in *Collected Poems.* Angus & Robertson, Sydney, 1972.

H.D. *Asphodel.* Duke University Press, Durham, 1992.

H.D. *Tribute to Freud.* Pantheon, New York, 1956.

Incognita. *The entombment of the Sibelles.* Paratext by D. Hecq.

Isodora. *The Negator of Miracles.* Paratext by D. Hecq.

Malroux, Claire. 'The wordless Woman' in *Birds and Bisons*, trans. M. Hacker. The Sheep Meadow Press Roverdale-on-Hudson, New York, 2004.

De Man, *The Resistance to Theory*. Manchester University Press, Manchester, 1986.

Minnette, Walter. *The Sculptress*. Pan Books, London, 1993.

Paré, Ambroise. 'A Surgeon in the Field' in Ross, J. B. and McLaughlin, M. (eds), *The Portable Renaissance Reader*, Penguin, Harmondsworth, 1977.

Peau d'âme. *Dreams*. Paratext by D. Hecq.

Rilke, Rainer Maria. *The Selected Poems*, Vintage, London, 1989.

Rimbaud, Arthur, 'A season in Hell' in Bernard, Oliver (trans.), *Collected Works*. Penguin, Harmondsworth, 1986.

Schreber. *Memoirs of my Nervous Illness*. New York Review, New York, 2000.

Smith, Patti, *Early Work 1970-1979*, W.W. Norton, New York, 1994.

Vesalius, Andreas, 'Anatomy and the Art of Medicine' in Ross, J. B. and McLaughlin, M. M. (eds), *The Portable Renaissance Reader*. Penguin, Harmonsdworth, 1977.

www.ingramcontent.com/pod-product-compliance
Lightning Source LLC
Chambersburg PA
CBHW031203090426
42736CB00009B/770